My Weird Writing Tips

Dan Gutman

Pictures by
Jim Paillot

HARPER
An Imprint of HarperCollins Publishers

This book is dedicated to you.*

My Weird Writing Tips

Text copyright © 2013 by Dan Gutman

Illustrations copyright © 2013 by Jim Paillot

All rights reserved. Printed in the United States of America.

No part of this book may be used or reproduced in any manner whatsoever without written permission except in the case of brief quotations embodied in critical articles and reviews. For information address HarperCollins Children's Books, a division of HarperCollins Publishers, 195 Broadway, New York, NY 10007.

www.harpercollinschildrens.com

Library of Congress Cataloging-in-Publication Data

Gutman, Dan.

  My weird writing tips / by Dan Gutman ; pictures by Jim Paillot. — 1st ed.

    p.   cm.

  ISBN 978-0-06-209107-9 (hardcover bdgs.) — ISBN 978-0-06-209106-2 (pbk.)

  1. English language—Composition and exercises—Juvenile literature.   I. Paillot, Jim, ill. II. Title.

PE1408.G95 2013   2012029985

808.042—dc23

Typography by Kate Engbring

18 19 20 BRR 10 9 8 7 6

❖

First Edition

*Yeah, you—the kid holding the book.

Table of Contents

A Note to the Reader

You probably have mixed feelings about picking up this book. On the one hand, you think it might be funny because you've read the My Weird School series. Maybe A.J., Andrea, Michael, Ryan, Alexia, and Neil the nude kid will torment the grown-ups at Ella Mentry School and a lot of silly stuff will go on.

On the other hand, it looks like this might be a book about *writing*. Ugh, disgusting! It's probably going to be a big borefest—one of those books your mom and dad want you to read because they think it will make you smarter or help you get better grades.

The truth is, it's both. You just might learn something, but you might get a few laughs too. So give it a shot. What have you got to lose? This just might be the greatest book in the history of the world.*

---

* When you see one of these asterisk thingies, look down. But you already know that or you wouldn't be reading this.

INTRODUCTION: DON'T BE A DUMBHEAD

You mean, like Andrea?

I'm not a dumbhead! I use perfectly correct grammar and spelling. If anyone is a dumbhead, it's you, Arlo.

Oh, yeah. I forgot to introduce A.J. and Andrea. They're two of my characters from the My Weird School series. They're going to help me talk about grammar.

Anyway, this is the part where I'm supposed to tell you why you need to read this book. Well, to be perfectly honest, you *don't*.

Nobody's going to throw you in jail if you don't use correct grammar and spelling. You don't *need* to write well to live. I've heard all the reasons for not learning how to write a million hundred times:

- None of my friends bother with punctuation and all that garbage. So why should I?

- I'm in a hurry. It's a busy world. Everything moves faster than it did back in the Dark Ages. Get with it, old man.

- When I text with my friends, I can only send a limited number of letters. So there's no point in learning how to write proper English.

- I communicate just fine right now. **CUL8R** is the same as **see you later**. **GR8** is the same as **great**. And I can write the short versions faster.

- This is how I stick it to The Man, or my parents, or my teachers, or old people who grew up before computers. And besides, anything a grown-up tells me to do has to be wrong.

- Spelling, grammar, and punctuation are boring.

- Being illiterate is cool. (Hey, some people really think this!)

Okay, I get it. You've decided to ignore the "rules" and just write whatever you want. I respect your independence. Now I'm going to tell you the one simple reason why you should change your mind. Are you ready? Here it is.

You sound like a dumbhead.

That's it. I said it. I didn't want to say it, but somebody had to. If your teacher gives you an assignment and you write, "I want to go over *their*," you sound like a dumbhead. If you write, "The *girls's* lined up in *sise* order," you sound like a dumbhead.

You don't want to sound like a dumbhead, do you? Sounding like a dumbhead isn't cool. And besides, dumbheads don't get into good colleges. They don't get good jobs.

I really shouldn't say that. Some dumbheads *do* get great jobs and make gobs of money. Maybe you can think of a few.

Call me a nerd if you want. I still think communication matters. And I think you

should too. That's why I wrote this book.
So don't be a dumbhead.

Now, let's get started.

Here are some things you will *not* learn
in this book, but would make good names
for rock bands:

The Gerunds

The Irregular Verbs

The Indefinite Articles

The Dangling Participles

The Split Infinitives

The Syntax

The Direct Objects

The Idioms

The Misplaced Modifiers

The Coordinating Conjunctions

I remember sitting in English class (that's what they called it back in prehistoric times) listening to Mrs. Zatzkus talk about subordinate clauses, nominatives, and subjunctive whatchamacallits. Well, you're not going to hear about any of that stuff in this book. Why not? Because I have no idea what any of those words mean. Oh, I tried to learn them, but it made no sense at all to me.

The good news is, it doesn't matter. You don't need to know *everything* to get your point across. I've written a hundred books, and I wouldn't know what a possessive pronoun was if it fell on my head.

In this book, you're not just going to learn a bunch of boring grammar rules. You're going to learn how to *communicate*. You're going to learn how to *write*.

"How vain it is to sit down to write when you have not stood up to live."
—Henry David Thoreau

PART I
TELLING A GOOD STORY

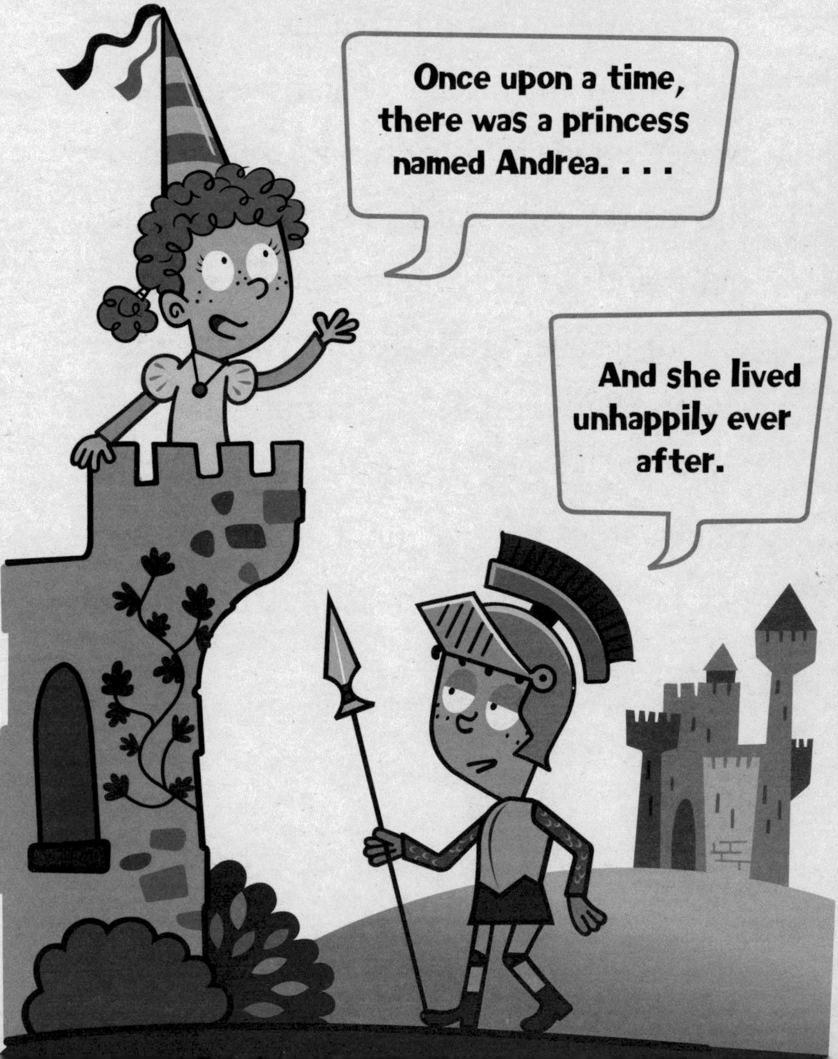

"Where do you get your ideas?"

★ ★ ★

This is the question that authors hear more than any other.* The answer is that we get our ideas from *everywhere*. We read the newspaper, watch TV, listen to the radio, and surf the internet.

Your teacher probably tells you to write about what you like and about what you know. That's exactly correct. Write about things that are meaningful to you. An old family story. A treasured object. A

---

* Well, except for, "Why do you have that bald spot on the back of your head?"

relative. An important moment in your life. The time you moved. An embarrassing event. Something you're afraid of. The *best* thing that ever happened to you. The *worst* thing that ever happened to you. A favorite pet, living or dead. That time you did that dumb thing and got into trouble.

Look for things that happened to you in real life, interesting people you've met, or weird things that went on at school. Observe the world around you. Keep an eye out for things that are unusual, funny, or different.

I'll add something to that. Don't just write about what you know. Write about what you *want to know*. Be curious.

When I visit a school, I usually have lunch with a group of kids like you. Sometimes, the kids are shy because they think they have nothing to say.

So I came up with a little trick. I ask, "Did any of you ever break a bone?" Instantly, all the hands shoot up.

Suddenly, everyone's competing to tell me a story. Ryan remembers the time he jumped off his bed and cracked his head open. Kaylee tells me about the time her brother drove the shopping cart into the ditch and spent the night in the hospital. Jules brings up the time he fell off his bike and . . . well, you get the idea.

Chances are, something very interesting happened to you at some point in your life. It just may be something worth writing about.

Carry a notebook with you wherever you go. Jot down ideas. If you don't have a notebook, write on a napkin. Write on a piece of wood. Write on your hand. Mark my words, if you don't write it down, you're going to forget that great idea.

I keep a diary. I hope Arlo never reads it. . . .

You probably write about flowers and butterflies in your diary.

"Writing comes more easily if you have something to say."
—*Sholem Asch*

What's the big idea?

★ ★ ★

What if nothing exciting ever happened to you? You never jumped off your bed and cracked your head open. You never ran a shopping cart into a ditch. You've led a completely boring and uneventful life What are you going to write about *then*?

Fear not! All hope is not lost! Even the most boring person in the history of the world has a great story to tell.

Take me, for example. Believe me, I'm really boring. I'm so boring that raking the leaves in my backyard may be the most exciting thing I do today. But when I write a book, I start with what I call "a big idea." I imagine an ordinary kid and put that kid into an extraordinary situation.

For example, what would happen if a kid ran for president of the United States? That simple idea led to my books *The Kid Who Ran for President* and *The Kid Who Became President*.

One day I thought, What would happen if a kid got the chance to take a basketball free throw, and if he made it he would win a million dollars? That led to my book *The Million Dollar Shot* (which led to *The Million Dollar Kick*, *The Million Dollar Goal*, *The Million Dollar Putt*, and *The Million Dollar Strike*).

Another time, I thought, What would

happen if a kid found the most valuable
baseball card in the world, and discovered
he had the power to travel through time
with it? That led to my book *Honus & Me*
(and eleven sequels that followed it). *My
Weird School* happened because I won-
dered, What would happen if there was
a school in which all the grown-ups were
crazy?

What if? What if? What if?

These are the kinds of stories I think kids like you can fantasize about. Maybe you can come up with a big "what if" idea of your own.

How to write a story from scratch

★ ★ ★

Okay, let's say you did all that stuff I suggested and you *still* don't have any ideas, big or small. You're in trouble, kid! Because one of these days, your teacher is going to say to the class, "Write a story."

Your mind will be a blank. Your brain will be paralyzed. You'll freak out. You'll peek over at the kid sitting next to you, figuring maybe you can copy something off her. But she's going to cover her paper so you can't see it. What are you going to do *then*?

Relax! I'm going to tell you how to write

a story from scratch, even if your brain fell out of your head.* We're going to write a story in half an hour, and it's going to be awesome. It's going to be fun, too. Trust me on this.

The first thing you need

Okay, what do you think is the first thing we need to write a cool story? The title, right?

Right!

WRONG!

Oh.
I knew that.

---

* In fact, having no brain may be to your advantage. . . .

How are you going to come up with a title if you don't even have any ideas?

No, the first thing you need is a *setting*. A setting is the geographic location where the story is going to take place. That's easy. You can set your story anywhere in the world. Chicago. Tokyo. London. Or out of the world. You could set it in outer space. You could set it inside a shoe. Or in your mouth. Use your imagination.

So let's say you chose the inside of a mouth as your setting. That's a little weird, but there's nothing wrong with weird. I can vouch for that.

Hi

The main character

The next thing we need for our story is a main character. No names yet. We just need an individual that we might find inside a mouth. A tooth, for example. Or a tongue. A germ, maybe. That's it! Our main character is going to be a germ.

Let's give our main character a name. You can call him or her anything you'd like. Since you're not here sitting with me as I write this, I'll call him Germany. Germany the Germ. Or Germy. That's catchy.

The goal or problem

In every story, the main character always has some kind of a goal he's trying to achieve, or a problem she's trying to solve.

So what kind of goal or problem can we give to a germ in somebody's mouth?

Maybe he wants to infect the body. That wouldn't be very nice. Maybe he wants to take over the world. Nah, that's been done a million times. Maybe he's a *nice* germ. Maybe he just wants to meet a nice girl germ and settle down with her in the back of the mouth and raise some bacteria together.

Can germs produce bacteria? Let's worry about that later. For now, in the idea stage, anything can happen.

Germs *are* bacteria. I found that out at the library.

Can you possibly be any more boring?

Secondary characters

Okay, let's continue. Germy the germ isn't going to be the only character in the story. There have to be at least a few *secondary* characters to interact with the main character. Secondary characters can be completely invented, or you can base them on people you know—the way they look, the way they speak, the way they burp all the time, whatever.

Germy's "girlfriend" has to be one of the secondary characters, of course. Maybe a talking tooth can be another. How about a uvula? Do you know what a uvula is? That's the thing that hangs in the back of your throat and looks like a punching bag. Uvulas are cool.

Okay, we have our characters now. Let's back up for a moment. Remember, our story is going to take place inside somebody's mouth. The main character is a germ named Germy. He wants to find the girl germ of his dreams. There's also a talking tooth and a uvula in the story.

Now, how do we begin?

Start with a bang!

When I write one of my books, I always try to start out with a **BANG**. I'll tell you why. I have a short attention span. If I open a book and the author doesn't grab me on the first page, I lose interest and close the book. That's just the way I am, and I think a lot of kids feel this way too. So we need to have something happen right off the bat that is *so* captivating that the reader will be dying to know what happens next.

Hmmm . . .

How about this? Germy is minding his own business when suddenly, there's a giant flood! Mouthwash comes pouring into the mouth. Germy is swept away. He's clinging to a tooth (the talking tooth, of course) for dear life! The mouthwash stings. Ouch! Oh, the horror!

"Hold on!" shouts the talking tooth. "I'll save you!"

That's exciting! If I picked up a book and on the first page a germ got swept away and was almost killed in a tsunami of mouthwash, I would want to know what happens next.

So what happens next?

Germy somehow survives the flood, of course, because he's our main character. It would be weird to kill off your main character on the first page. Your job is to figure out a way for Germy to get out of this jam.

Let's say that when the waters subside, there's this really pretty girl germ who is passed out on the middle of the tongue. She's barely alive. Germy rushes over and nurses her back to health.

Now, it would be very easy to say the girl germ is so grateful that she vows to marry Germy and they both live happily ever after.

But wait! What about . . . the evil uvula!

Oh yeah, I forgot to mention that the uvula is the bad guy in the story. It's always fun to have a character who is a bad guy. The uvula hates Germy because . . . he's prejudiced against germs. That's it! And he's determined to stop Germy no matter what.

What happens next?

I'm not going to tell you.

Okay, okay, I'll tell you.

No, I won't! *You* decide what happens next! Hey, I'm not going to write the whole thing for you. You've got a better imagination than I do, because you're a kid and I'm just an old fart who has to use a little machine to trim my nose hairs.

The point is that it's *easy* to write a story even if you have no ideas. . . .

STORYTELLING CHECKLIST

☐ First, pick a setting, any geographic location that interests you. Find out about your setting. Do a little research about it, so you can sprinkle in a few facts here and there.

☐ Think of a main character that suits your setting. It doesn't *have* to be human. In fact, it doesn't even have to be alive.

☐ Do a little research to make your story come to life. If you were writing the story we just started, you might want to go online and look up how many germs are in a human mouth. Look up how long a germ can live. Do they move? Do they grow? Do they have any humanlike qualities? You can use this information to make your characters and story more interesting.

☐ Give your main character a goal to achieve or a problem to solve. The more outrageous, the better.

☐ Surround your main character with a few interesting and unusual secondary characters. A secondary character could be an ally (like Robin in *Batman*). It could be a teacher (like Obi-Wan Kenobi in *Star Wars*). It could be a clown who provides comic relief (like Donkey in *Shrek*). Or it could be a villain (like Dr. Evil in *Austin Powers*). Actually, bad guys are the most fun to write, I must admit.*

☐ Start with a bang. The first sentence in your story needs to grab the reader's attention. Have something unusual, unexpected, or amazing happen.

---

* You can make them do all kinds of outrageous stuff and, in the end, kill them off in a really interesting way. That's always fun.

☐ Next comes the most important and fun part: let your imagination go wild!

☐ And just like you started off the story with a bang, try to finish with one too. It doesn't always have to be a happy ending, but it should be a satisfying one. Better yet, a surprise ending. Blow the reader's mind!

Writer's block

It happens to everybody. At some point, you're going to get stuck. You won't know what should happen next. What can you do about it?

Here's a little trick—have something *bad* happen to your main character.

I'm serious. Don't worry about being nice to your characters. What did they ever do for you? Nothing!

Be nice to people in the *real* world. In a story, the author can do *anything* to the characters, and there's nothing they can do about it. They're fictional!

In my Baseball Card Adventure series, I have had my main character get screamed at, chased by a lunatic with a baseball bat, kidnapped, tied to a chair, and shot. So go ahead. Break your main character's leg. Have her get caught in a tornado. Let an evil genius from a parallel universe suck his brain out through his nose. It's up to you.

Throw an obstacle in your main character's path.* It will make your story more

---

* Make it a big one, out of concrete.

exciting, and your character will grow and become more interesting and realistic. Just like in real life. Bad things happen to good people. They have to deal with it.

"No matter how sweet and innocent your leading characters, make awful things happen to them."
—Kurt Vonnegut

The title

Finally, your story is finished. It doesn't matter if it came out to one page or a hundred. You wrote a story, and you should be proud of yourself.

Remember a few pages back when I asked you what was the first thing you'd need, and you said, "The title"? Well, now is the time to come up with a title. Think of an irresistible title that people will be anxious to read. *The Adventures of Germy the Germ. Germy Falls in Love. Germy Mouths Off. Germ Warfare. Weapons of Mouth Destruction.* Whatever. Try to keep it short, and descriptive.

I once wrote a book about a kid who

was a Hollywood stuntman. He was always falling out of windows and getting set on fire. To this day, I think it is my best book. My son, Sam, told me I should title it *The Stunt Kid*. I ignored him and titled it *Johnny Hangtime*. I told Sam that Mark Twain didn't title his book *The Kid Who Floated Down the River on a Raft*. He titled it *Huckleberry Finn*. Sam replied, "You're not Mark Twain."

He was right. The book didn't sell very well. I should have titled it *The Stunt Kid*.

So now you know how to write a story even if you have no ideas at all. And you know what? You don't even have to wait for your teacher to give you an assignment. Just write a story for the fun of it. You may come up with something great. You may be the next Dr. Seuss. You may be the next J. K. Rowling.

The best part is that when you write a story, *you're* in charge. You, and only you, get to decide what's going to happen to those characters. That's the power you have as the author. It's a great feeling to be in control like that, and great fun too. It's like creating your own little world.

"If there's a book you really want to read, but it hasn't been written yet, then you must write it."
—Toni Morrison

You're going to hate this part

Okay, your story is done. What should you do now? Go to Disney World? No! The next thing you need to do is . . .

WRITE THE WHOLE THING ALL OVER AGAIN!

WHAT?

I know, you hate me now. You worked really hard on your story. You wrote the thing. It's finished, it's perfect, and you don't want to change a word. But you know what? Professional writers revise a manuscript *over and over* again until it is as good as they can make it.

Why? Because we messed up the first time. Everybody does. Your first draft may be good, but it can be better. Some of the wording may be clumsy. Some of the sentences may be out of order. There's always room for improvement.

Bummer in the summer!

That's right. But don't despair. Read the next section. . . .

"I'm not a very good writer, but I'm an excellent rewriter."
—James Michener

My little secret
. . . .

Here's a trick I use to improve my writing. I'm pretty sure I invented it. Maybe not. In any case, I never heard of anybody else who uses it.

I shouldn't be revealing this secret to you, because once everybody finds out, any dumbhead will be able to do what I do. But I'm going to tell you anyway, because this book is dedicated to you, and you seem like a good kid. So keep it to yourself, okay? I've got enough competition as it is.

Here's the trick—after you finish your first draft, let it sit there and "age" for a while. A couple of days, at least. It will fade, just a little bit, in your memory. Next, pick it up again and read it **OUT LOUD** while you **PRETEND TO BE SOMEBODY ELSE**.

It's as simple as that. Pretend to be your teacher, a parent, your best friend, or a complete stranger.

When you read the words out loud and pretend to be somebody else, it's almost

You can pretend to be me, Arlo!

Ugh, disgusting!

like you're reading those words through someone else's eyes. You'll see the mistakes you made the first time. You'll see where you can make the writing better, clearer, and sharper.

Yes, people may think you're crazy while you're reading out loud. But maybe they think that anyway.

As you read it out loud, the words should flow smoothly in your mind. One word should lead naturally to the next one. One sentence should lead to the next one. One paragraph should lead to the next one. If the words don't sound right in your mind, they're not right. Make some changes so the whole thing flows.

My goal is to write books that flow so smoothly that after two hours you'll look up and think, "Wow! That didn't even feel like I was reading! I felt like I was watching a movie in my head."

That's my secret. Now rip this book into a million little pieces so nobody else finds out.

Well, don't rip it into a million pieces if you bought the e-book version. That would be weird.

"A good style should show no signs of effort. What is written should seem a happy accident."
—W. Somerset Maugham

More secret tips. Shhhhh! Don't tell anyone!

Nobody gets it exactly right the first time! Every good story goes through at least one round of changes and corrections. Here are a few things to think about while you're writing and revising your story. . . .

Revising Your Story

★ ★ ★

Break it up!

When I read essays written by kids, there's one problem that jumps out over and over again: You don't use paragraphs!

I don't get it. Some of my best friends are paragraphs. They're harmless. In fact, they add a lot to your writing by spacing out your thoughts.

So break it up. Look for natural places where the topic changes, even slightly. Bang! Put a new paragraph right there. Your paragraphs don't have to be long. They can even be one sentence.

Like this—here's a paragraph right *here*!

A paragraph can even be one *word* long.

See?

But don't overdo it, okay?

It.

Would.

Be.

Obnoxious.

To.

Write.

Paragraphs.

Like.

This.

The important thing is, a paragraph should *not* be a full page or longer. Unless, of course, you want to see your reader's head explode.

Are you allergic?

Some kids appear to be allergic to periods.
I can't think of any other reason why they
refuse to use them. See if you enjoy reading this:

> *Jimmy and I went to the store and got*
> *some Slim Jims and then we came home*
> *and hung out in my basement and then*

we played some video games and did our homework and this guy rang the bell and tried to get us to donate money for some charity and then his mom called and said he had to come home so he went home and that was pretty much what happened today.

Or would you rather read this?

Jimmy and I went to the store. We got some Slim Jims and then we came home and hung out in my basement. We played some video games and then we did our homework. This guy rang the bell and tried to get us to donate money for some charity. Jimmy's mom called and said he had to come home. So he went home. That was pretty much what happened today.

Admittedly, neither of those paragraphs is going to win the Nobel Prize or anything.

That's a prize they give out to people who don't have bells.

But at least the second one is readable. It was broken down into short, simple, easy-to-read chunks. The first one is a long run-on sentence.

There's no extra charge for using periods, folks. So use 'em. Put one thought in each sentence, not ten. Run-on sentences are boring.

How not to bore people to death

If I ask a hundred reluctant readers why they don't like to read, almost all of them will reply, "Because it's boring."

People get bored incredibly easily. I once fell asleep while watching one of the *Mission: Impossible* movies. You've got to be *really* easily bored for that to happen.

You don't want to bore anybody with your writing. So how can you avoid that?

Trim the fat

Did you ever hear the expression "less is more"? You may think you're fooling your teacher by using a page and a half to describe the beautiful sunset you witnessed on your summer vacation.

Look, I hate to tell you this, but nobody cares. Your teacher isn't going to give you an A because you wrote something that was twice as long as what the kid sitting next to you wrote. Your teacher has twenty-five or thirty of these papers to read. She doesn't want to go home after school and spend hours reading a page and a half about your sunset. She wants to go to her aerobics class. She wants to watch a movie on HBO. She wants to work on her stamp collection.

Does anybody still collect stamps?

Anyway, you're going to put your teacher to sleep if you go on for page after page describing a sunset, or what somebody's face looks like, or the way somebody holds an umbrella. Move it along. Get to the point. You don't want your readers to die from old age while they're reading your story.

Look over the first draft of something

you've written. Now, see how many words you can cut out, while still keeping the meaning. For every word you can get rid of, treat yourself to an M&M. (No fair putting in extra words so you can cut them out later and get more M&M's.) If that doesn't work, pretend there's an ink shortage. Pretend each word costs you a dollar. Cut! Cut! Cut!

Kill the adjectives!

An adjective is a word that describes a noun. Like *big* describes *whale*. But *all* whales are big, so there's no need to write *big whale*.

Some people will tell you that you should pile on the adjectives to make your story more vivid (or simply longer). Well, how does *this* sound?

> *The tall, blond, handsome, tired, gawky ten-year-old boy was wearing a new, bright red, flannel shirt as he walked down the dark, forbidding cobblestone street. . . .*

ZZZZZZZZZZZZZZZ

Oh, sorry, I dozed off there for a moment. Look, who cares what the kid was wearing? What difference does it make what kind of stones were in the street? Get rid of that boring stuff! Get that kid to wherever it is he's going, have something *cool* happen there, and move the story along. You don't have to mention *every* detail along the way. Readers have imaginations. Let them use them.

Elmore Leonard, a very famous author for adults, uses the word *hooptedoodle* to describe all the boring stuff that is found in so many books. As Leonard puts it, "I try to leave out the part(s) that readers tend to skip." You don't want to read hooptedoodle, so don't write hooptedoodle.

I could go on and on talking about this subject, but I would be doing exactly what I've been telling you not to do. I think you get the point with three words—trim the fat.

"As to the Adjective:
when in doubt, strike it out."
—Mark Twain

A few words about reading

I've been telling you that writing should be simple, to the point, and effortless to read. But not all books are like that. In fact, many of the books you may have to read for school are just the opposite.

If you struggle to read a book, it doesn't mean you're dumb or a poor reader. It just means that book is intended for a different kind of person. Some people *like* to read stories that are very complicated, with long passages of "word pictures" describing the way people look, the way a flower smells, or what the weather is like. Other people prefer stories that get straight to the action and leave the rest to the reader's imagination. As they say, different strokes for different folks.

"Never use a long word when a diminutive one will do."
—William Safire

Dialogue—

a fancy word

for talking

"People like to talk," said Andrea Young, this annoying girl with curly brown hair, "and readers like to read about characters talking."

"Why do you think that is?" said her equally annoying crybaby friend Emily.

"Well," said Andrea, "dialogue livens up the story, and it also breaks up the text on the page with a little white space."

"So I should try to have some dialogue in my story?" said Emily.

"Sure," said Andrea. "That is, if the characters have anything worth saying."*

Set off dialogue using quotation marks. Use commas between the quotation marks and the part about who is doing the talking.

"I'm awesome," I said.

---

* This is the kind of conversation Andrea and Emily have when nobody's around.

He said, she said, they said, you said, we said

Did you notice in that last section that the word *said* was used every time Andrea or Emily said something? The problem is that *said* gets to be boring after reading it a few times in a row.

You don't always have to use that word. There are plenty of other ways to say *said*, and they're more descriptive. You'll find a lot more if you go online and search for "other ways to say said" but here are some examples:

added   *cried*   *pleaded*

admitted   **declared**   proclaimed

agreed

announced

ARGUED

asked

babbled

barked

begged

BELLOWED

boasted

bragged

called

COMMENTED

drawled

exclaimed

EXPLAINED

gasped

growled

grumbled

GRUNTED

HOLLERED

insisted

joked

mumbled

MUTTERED

quipped

remarked

replied

responded

ROARED

SHOUTED

sighed

snapped

sputtered

stammered

suggested

whispered

YELLED

Nonfiction:
keeping it real

★ ★ ★

So far, we've been talking about writing fiction. But your teacher may ask you to write a nonfiction essay about something you're studying in class.

Writing nonfiction is different from writing fiction, of course. You can't just make up any old crazy stuff in your head. You've got to stick with the facts. But there are a lot of similarities, too. You still want to tell a story in nonfiction. You're just telling a *true* story.

Let's say your topic is alligators. The first step should be to gather a bunch of facts. Try to find out everything you can about alligators. See if there are any books about them in your school library or the public library. Check the encyclopedia. Go online and search for "alligators." Try to find a movie about alligators.

While you're looking at all this material, make a note of any fact about alligators that captures your interest. If it interests you, it will probably be interesting to other people, too.

When I'm researching a book, I jot down interesting facts on three-by-five-inch index cards—one note on each card. I may have a stack of two hundred cards by the time I'm finished researching. You may want to try this card system with your writing too. It's a really simple way to organize your information.

When you feel that you've gathered enough information, the next step is to organize it. Read through your cards one by one, sorting the cards into groups that seem to go together. Start to make smaller piles of cards on the floor. You might have a pile of cards about what alligators eat, a pile about where they live, a pile about what they look like, and so on. Basically, you're taking a big topic (alligators) and breaking it down into smaller pieces.

Next, take those piles and put them into an order that tells a story—a true story—about alligators. Explain where they live, what they look like, how they behave, what they eat, and so on.

Just like in a fiction story, you still want to start with a bang to grab the reader's attention. (Maybe there was a famous alligator attack?) You still want to break the story up into lots of sentences and paragraphs. You still want to cut the hooptedoodle. And of course, you still need to rewrite the story to make it as good as it can be.

Getting published
★ ⋆ ★

I know what you're thinking. You wrote a story. You think it's pretty good. Now you want to send it to *me* so I can help you get it published.

No! Don't! I'm not a publisher.* But the good news is that there are lots of places— especially online—that accept writing by kids. The following list includes just a few. Your teacher or librarian may be able to help you find more.

---

* Hey, I have a tough enough time getting my *own* stuff published.

- **Stone Soup.** A print and web magazine written by kids from eight to thirteen. (www.stonesoup.com)

- **DiaryLand.** Create your own diary. (http://members.diaryland.com/edit/welcome.phtml)

- **The Telling Room.** A program dedicated to young writers to honor the act of storytelling. (www.tellingroom.org)

- **Tikatok.** Enables kids to create their own books online (including pictures) and actually have them printed and mailed to them. (www.tikatok.com)

PART 2
HOW TO RITE IT WRIGHT.
I MEAN WRITE IT RIGHT.

The Parts of Speech

★ ★ ★

Okay, so I won't go too far into the parts of speech, because there are a lot of rules to learn and they can bog you down when you're writing if you think too much about them.

Basically, a **NOUN** is a person, place, or thing. It either does something, in which case it's called a *subject*, or it receives something, in which case it's called an *object*.

A **VERB** is an action word, like *run*, *jump*, or *play*.

An **ADJECTIVE** describes a noun, like

tall, **blue**, or **pretty**. We'll talk more about adjectives later.

An **ADVERB** describes a verb, saying *how* you did something (it even has the word *verb* in it so you can remember). Adverbs are words like **quickly**, **politely**, and **happily**, and usually end in **-ly**.

Finally, **PREPOSITIONS** are words that show the relationship between things. You know a word is a preposition if it fits into one of these two sentences:

- *Everyone is tired _____ Mr. Granite's class. (for example, **of**, **from**, **with**, **in**)*
- *The squirrel went _____ the tree. (for example, **to**, **for**, **after**, **into**, **up**, **around**)*

Witch should you use? I mean, which.

It's or Its?

One of the biggest problems in the history of the world is when to write *its* and when to write *it's* in a sentence. This problem has been around for centuries.

In fact, most people don't know this, but when Cain and Abel were born, Eve printed up baby announcements that said, "Its a boy!" Adam took one look at them and said, "You dumbhead! That should be, 'It's a boy!'" They had to send all the announcements back and have them printed over again, which cost a pretty penny.

Actually, I made that whole thing up. It didn't happen. Adam and Eve didn't speak English, and they didn't have baby announcements or printing companies back then.

The point is, a lot of people have trouble

with *it's* and *its*.

Well, it's simple. Notice I didn't write *its* simple. That's because *it's simple* is just a less formal way of writing *it* is *simple*. You stick an apostrophe in there to take the place of the *i* in *is*. Any time you're changing *it is* (or *it has*) to *it's*, you throw an apostrophe in there.

And that's the *only* time you write *it's*.

Got that? Let me say it again. You *only* use an apostrophe when you are changing *it is* or *it has* to *it's*. As in:

· **It's** *a shame that Mr. Klutz parachuted onto our big pizza.*

- **It's** *weird that Officer Spence stole the peanut butter and jelly sandwiches.*
- **It's** *hilarious when Mr. Granite tells us to open our math books and then we get called to an assembly.*

You get the idea. If you hear the *it is* in your head, you should use an apostrophe.* Any *other* time you use "its," there

---

* And if you hear *it is* in your head, you should go to the doctor and get it checked out.

is *no* apostrophe. Got that? So you would write:

- *Ella Mentry School is famous for **its** weird teachers.*
- *Mrs. Yonkers turned on the computer and **its** screen was blank.*
- *A.J. shot a rubber band at the Barbie doll and **its** head fell off.*

If you're still confused about when to use *it's* or *its* in a sentence, just make sure to have somebody look over the baby announcements before you send them to the printers. That will solve the problem.

Lie or Lay?

I get this one wrong all the time. (Thank goodness I have editors to correct my writing!) When Neil the nude kid goes to

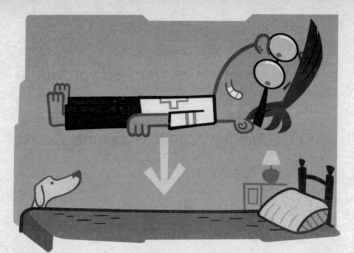

sleep, he will *lie* down on his bed. When he puts his backpack in his cubby, he will *lay* it down. You *lay* things down, but you *lie* down. You lay objects. People lie.

Can or May?

When you ask if you *may* do something, you're asking permission to do it. When you ask if you *can* do something, you're asking if you have the *ability* to do it.

So if Ryan wanted to ask Mr. Granite for permission to go to the bathroom, he would say, "May I go to the bathroom?" If he said, "Can I go to the bathroom?" he would be suggesting that he might be constipated.

Who or Whom?

Knock-knock.

Who's there?

To.

To who?

No, to *whom*.

Basically, *who* does something, while *whom* has something done to it.

I know, that's still not clear. With *who* and *whom*, probably the best thing to do is to read some examples of each until your ear is tuned to what sounds right. A few examples of *who*:

- **Who** *invented the telephone?*
- **Who** *ate my candy?*
- **Who** *loves ya, baby?*
- *Mr. Klutz,* **who** *has no hair at all, came into our class.*
- *Roger Daltrey was a member of The* **Who**.

And some examples of *whom*:

- *To* **whom** *am I speaking?*
- *To* **whom** *it may concern.*
- *With* **whom** *did you go to the dance?*
- *To* **whom** *were you talking?*
- *There were four guys, one of* **whom** *was the leader.*

Those words *to*, *with*, and *of* are called **PREPOSITIONS**. So *whom* is the word you use if it's an object of a preposition, while *who* is the word you use if it's a subject.

Wow, Arlo, I'm impressed!

I'm not in the gifted-and-talented program for nothing.

Honestly, I don't really understand *who* or *whom* either. When in doubt, stick with *who*. *Whom* sounds a little old-fashioned and formal, like you're having a spot of tea with the queen of England. If you start throwing around a lot of *whom*s with the guys at the playground, they'll probably beat you up and take your lunch money.

Me or I?

The titles of my Baseball Card Adventure books are *Honus & Me, Jackie & Me, Babe & Me,* and so on. About once a year, I'll be at a book signing and some smarty-pants kid will raise a hand and say, "The titles to your books are grammatically incorrect. They should be *Honus & I, Babe & I . . .*"

My response is to shout, "Security! Get that kid outta here!"

But seriously, when to use *me* and when to use *I* is one of those problems that just about *everybody* has, kids and adults. So don't feel bad if you mess it up.

Most of the time, when you use the wrong word, it *sounds* weird. You would never write "He likes I," "Me don't want that," "Give it to I," or "He punched I." (Unless, of course, you were writing a story about Tarzan. He would always introduce himself by saying "Me Tarzan." It would sound weird if he said "My name is Tarzan.")

Take this sentence: Michael and I walked to school together.

"Michael and me" would sound a little weird.

In other situations, *me* or *I* isn't so

obvious. "Me and A.J. went to school" sounds fine to my ear. But it's wrong. The correct way to say it is, "A.J. and I went to school."

How do you know? Try this. Say the sentence both ways:

- *"A.J. and I went to school."*
- *"A.J. and me went to school."*

Now, leave out A.J. and see if it makes sense:

- *"I went to school."*
- *"Me went to school."*

The second one sounds obviously wrong. So "A.J. and I went to school" is correct.

That doesn't mean that "and I" is *always* correct. "Come with A.J. and I" sounds okay. But you wouldn't say "Come with I," so you shouldn't say, "Come with A.J. and I." In that case, it should be "Come with A.J. and *me*."

It's complicated, I know.

I is almost always the subject, while *me* is always an object. It can be the object of a preposition, like "Give that candy *to me*," or it can be the object of a verb, like "Andrea *poked me*."

Did not!

The nice thing is that as you grow older and gain more experience reading and hearing people speak, your ear is going to naturally tune in to what sounds right and what sounds wrong. Most of the time, if something sounds right when you read it out loud, it *is* right.

Your brain and ears are terrific editors. When they hear a sentence that has been written poorly, they know. It sounds weird. It looks weird. Even if you don't know the rules, you can tell that something is off. Bad writing almost always sounds weird.

But every so often, bad grammar, punctuation, and spelling look or sound just fine. As you get older, your teachers (who are way smarter than I am) are going to teach you the more complicated rules of grammar. You're going to learn about double negatives, active and passive voice, tenses, and all that other fun stuff from your language arts teacher. For now, just make sure the words sound right in your head.

Let's try a few more difficult words.

You're or Your?

You're is simply another way to say *you are*. As in: "You think you are (you're) pretty smart, Andrea. But actually, you are (you're) a dumbhead."

Say the sentence you are (you're)

thinking of out loud. If you can't hear the words *you are* in there, do not use *you're*.

Your refers to something that belongs to you:

- *Why would you poke **your** head into a door?*
- *None of **your** beeswax.*
- *So is **your** face.*
- *Run for **your** lives!*

They're, Their, or There?

Similarly, *they're* is just another way to say *they are*. As in: "Ms. Jafee and Mrs. Yonkers were doing jumping jacks in the teachers' lounge. They are (they're) weird! But they are (they're) getting good exercise."

Again, say your sentence out loud. If

you can't hear the words *they are*, don't use *they're*.

Their refers to something that two or more people own:

- *Andrea and Emily picked up **their** backpacks and stormed out of the vomitorium in a huff. They didn't even eat **their** lunches.*

There usually indicates a place:

- *Mrs. Yonkers was in the computer*

room, so Ryan and I went over **there**.

There is also used to indicate that something exists, or to mention it for the first time:

- **There** *is a half-pipe in Mr. Klutz's living room.*
- **There** *is no apostrophe in* **there**.

They're, their, and **there** are really quite easy. Just remember this: **There** is no reason why Ryan and Michael put straws in **their** noses. **They're** weird.

To, Too, or Two?

Two is a number: A.J. has *two* arms, *two* legs, and *two* nostrils.

Too means more than enough: Emily cries *too* much. Ryan ate *too* many hot dogs. *Too* can also mean *also*: We let Alexia come with us *too*.

To is used in all other cases.

Effect or Affect?

Affect is a verb. *Effect* is a noun. Remember, a noun is a thing and a verb is an action. So:

- *A.J.'s insults had an **effect** on Andrea.*
- *Adding more potatoes had no **effect** on the speed of Mr. Docker's car.*
- *I didn't think Mr. Tony's flamethrower would **affect** the pizza so quickly.*

- *Losing his hair did not **affect** Mr. Klutz. He just shaved the rest off.*
- *The **effect** of studying will **affect** your test score in a good way.*

Effect is used more frequently, so when in doubt, *effect* is effective!

Than or then?

Then is about time, and the order in which events take place:

- *A.J. bothered Andrea for a while, and **then** he bothered Emily.*
- *Miss Small juggled scarves, and **then** she made us do square dancing.*

Than is used to compare things:

- *Miss Lazar has more toilet-bowl plungers **than** anybody.*

- *Dr. Brad is a better Ping-Pong player* **than** *Ms. Coco.*

Punctuation: A Matter of Life and Death

★ ★ ★

Believe it or not, a punctuation mark can mean the difference between life and death. Take this example:

- *"Let's eat Cousin Richard!"*

That doesn't sound very nice, does it? You're saying you want to *eat* Cousin Richard! But if you stick one little comma in there, it means something completely different:

- *"Let's eat, Cousin Richard!"*

Now you're telling Cousin Richard that it's time to eat.

So punctuation is really a matter of life and death. At least for Cousin Richard.

The lovely comma

I admit it. I love commas. For years, I kept this secret. I didn't want anyone to know. I was ashamed. But I don't care anymore. I want to tell the world. I love commas!

There, I said it. I feel like such a burden has been lifted off my shoulders.

Commas are like a short rest in the middle of a sentence—like a time-out in the middle of a football game. Like a batter stepping out of the batter's box between pitches. Can you hear the pause after the comma in the following sentences?

Mr. Klutz held up his hand and made a peace sign, which means shut up.

After we finished pledging the

allegiance, we went to the all-purpose room for an assembly.

Stuff like that happens all the time, you know.

If those guys weren't my best friends, I would hate them.

Emily was on the floor, freaking out.

Ryan threw A.J.'s action figure out the window of the school bus, and it got run over.

A comma is also used to separate three or more items in a list. So:

- *A.J., Andrea, Michael, and Ryan went trick-or-treating together.*
- *They got Kit Kats, Twix bars, some Almond Joys, and a few Twizzlers.*

Periods

So if a comma is a short rest in the middle of a sentence, a period is a longer rest. A nap, you might say. When a thought comes to an end, you should put in a period there and start the next thought with a new sentence. Look at this paragraph:

My friend Neil, who we call the nude kid even though he wears clothes, has a pet ferret. Its name is Mr. Wiggles. Last year, Neil brought Mr. Wiggles to school on Crazy Pet Day. It escaped from its cage and climbed into a hat that belonged to

this crybaby girl named Emily—while it was on her head! Emily freaked and went running out of the room.

There were five thoughts in that paragraph.

1. Neil has a ferret.

2. The ferret's name is Mr. Wiggles.

3. Neil brought Mr. Wiggles to school.

4. Mr. Wiggles escaped.

5. Emily freaked out.

That paragraph could have been one really long run-on sentence. To make it easier to read, I put each thought in its own sentence. Periods separate the five thoughts.

Question marks

Huh?

You use a question mark at the end of any sentence that asks a question.* That's all I have to say about question marks.

Exclamation points

Use an exclamation point at the end of a sentence that is *amazing*. Such as:

- *It was the worst thing to happen since TV Turnoff Week!*
- *Bummer in the summer!*
- *What a crybaby!*
- *You should have* been *there!*
- *"WOW!" everybody said, which is MOM upside down.*
- *"I invented a new food!" Ms. LaGrange told us.*

---

* Thank you, Captain Obvious!

- *"Oh, snap!" said Ryan.*
- *"Freeze, dirtbags!" shouted Officer Spence.*

You wouldn't put an exclamation point at the end of a sentence like, "I went to the store." It would have to be some *really* amazing store for you to write, "I went to the store!" Or maybe, if the store was a million hundred miles from your house, it would be pretty amazing to go there and it might deserve an exclamation point. But why would you go to a store that was so far away when you could just go to a store in your town? That would be weird.

Anyway, try not to overdo it with

exclamation points. Sure, it's fun to hold a key down on the computer and see what happens (!!!!!!!!!!!!!!!!!!!!!!!). But that looks weird. And if you end *every* sentence with an exclamation point, the amazing thing you're writing about doesn't seem all that amazing anymore.

It's sort of like drinking a milk shake. That first sip sure tastes great. But after drinking ten milk shakes, you want to throw up.

"Keep your exclamation points under control."
—Elmore Leonard

Quotation marks

"Quotation marks are used at the beginning and end of someone's spoken words," said Andrea Young.

"I knew that," A.J. lied.

"You did not, Arlo!" shouted Andrea. "You probably also don't know that periods and commas go *inside* quotation marks. They should not go outside."

"Your *face* shouldn't go outside," A.J. said, "because it's ugly."

"You're mean!"

"I do know one thing about quotation marks," A.J. told Andrea.

"What is it?" she replied, rolling her eyes.

"Quotation marks are like pants."

"How is that, Arlo?"

"They always come in pairs," said A.J.

"You're a dumbhead."

"Why can't a truck full of quotation marks fall on your head?"

Apostrophes

Ah, the humble apostrophe! It's a funny-looking thing, isn't it? Funny-sounding thing too. So misunderstood (and hard to spell). Who would think that a simple little mark would cause so much trouble?

An apostrophe is often used to show that somebody *owns* something. Usually, you add an apostrophe and an s at the end of the name:

- *It was Andrea's dictionary.*

- *Ryan's mom is weird.*

If the name ends with an *s* (like Dr. Carbles), you should also stick on an apostrophe and an *s*:

- *We went over Dr. Carbles's house.*

Here's where things get tricky. In some cases, you just add an apostrophe with *no s*:

- *The girls' science project.*
- *The students' cubbies.*

You'll be able to tell when to do this because those phrases would sound a little weird if they had *another s* added to the end: *Girls's. Students's.*

Often, kids think they need to add an apostrophe to make a word plural. As in: I have two dog's. **DON'T DO THAT**! It's wrong! It looks weird too. You see that problem in grocery stores all the time: Apple's for sale. Egg's. Frozen food's. Anybody who adds an apostrophe and an s to make a word plural should be arrested by Officer Spence and sent to jail.

An apostrophe is also used to make a contraction. Remember when we discussed *it's* and *they're*? The apostrophe is put in the place of the missing letters when you put two words together.

Here are a bunch of common contractions, and sentences to help you remember them:

can't—cannot (Miss Daisy *can't* read or write.)

could've—could have (Mr. Klutz *could've* worn a toupee to cover his bald head.)

didn't—did not (Ms. Hannah *didn't* want to throw anything away.)

don't—do not (I *don't* understand Mrs. Kormel because she speaks her own language.)

how's—how is (*How's* Miss Child going to get the animals back into their cages?)

I'll—I will ("*I'll* fix the coffee machine," said Mr. Harrison.)

I'm—I am (*I'm* not feeling well, so *I'm* going to see Mrs. Cooney.)

isn't—is not (Ryan will eat anything, even stuff that *isn't* food.)

it's—it is (It's best you just remember this one!)

let's—let us (*Let's* go see Mr. Hynde perform in concert.)

she's—she is (Miss Small fell out of a tree. *She's* accident-prone.)

shouldn't—should not (Andrea thinks kids *shouldn't* say inappropriate words like *butt* and *dumbhead*.)

that's—that is (*That's* the first rule of being a kid.)

wasn't—was not (Miss Lazar *wasn't* there, so we couldn't fix the toilets.)

what's—what is (*What's* for lunch, Ms. LaGrange?)

who's—who is (*Who's* going to repair Mr. Sunny's sand castle?)

won't—will not (Mrs. Roopy *won't* admit that she's the librarian.)

Apostrophes can get confusing because they are sometimes used in other situations (*the 1960's, always dot your i's and cross your t's, learn your ABC's, go get 'em*).

But with a little practice and common sense, you'll understand when to use an apostrophe, and when to leave it out.

Spelling: Noing Rite frum Rong
I mean knowing right from wrong.

★ ★ ★

I know, I know.

I saved this part until now because I know how hard it is, and how much some of you hate it. A lot of kids (there's no such word as *alot*, by the way) think that in the age of texting and tweeting, nobody needs to spell words correctly anymore.

It's true. You can just tap out any old letters on your keyboard or keypad. But when you go to school and write *enuf* in an essay when you mean *enough*, you're going to look like a dumbhead. (And like I said before, you're also not going to get good grades or make the big bucks.)

English is a weird language

A long time ago, some imbecile decided that we should spell the word *through* like this: **T-H-R-O-U-G-H**. What could he (I assume it was a guy) have been thinking? It was probably the same guy who came up with the idea of putting peanut butter and jelly in the same jar. Think of how many hours humanity would have saved over the centuries if that dumbhead had simply spelled the word like this: T-H-R-U. Why, I bet we would all have flying cars and jet packs by now.

Spelling is really hard, because English is such a weird language. Sometimes a word can look right (rite?), but is completely wrong (rong?). Sometimes it looks wrong (wrong?) but is completely right (right?). In a perfect world, *right* would (wood?) be spelled *rite*, and *wrong* should be spelled *rong*. Right?

Sometimes English just makes no sense at all.

Vegetarians eat vegetables, but humanitarians don't eat humans (that I know of, anyway). How can a bass be a fish and also a kind of guitar? We recite at a play and play at a recital. We drive on the parkway and park on the driveway.

A slim chance and a fat chance are the exact same thing. You fill *in* a form the same way you fill *out* a form, and your alarm is just as annoying whether it goes *off* or *on*. If your house burns *up* or burns *down*, you still end up with no house. Our noses run and our feet smell instead of the other way around.

The plural of *goose* is *geese*, and the plural of *tooth* is *teeth*. So why isn't the plural of *booth beeth* and *moose meese*? Or *mooses*? How can one deer be called a deer, and a hundred deer be . . . deer?

What's up with that?

A bandage can be *wound* around a *wound*. A farm can *produce*

produce. Polish people *polish* furniture. There's no time like the *present* to *present* someone with a *present.* You can *object* to an *object.* You can be too *close* to a door to *close* it. If the *wind* is too strong, you could *wind* up dead. If you *tear* up a paper, it could bring a *tear* to your eye.

Why is quicksand slow? Why are boxing rings square? And for goodness' sake, can somebody tell me why there are no eggs in eggplant, no ham in hamburger, and no dogs in hot dogs?

Well, I know why there are no dogs in hot dogs. Because nobody would eat

them! But you get the point. In far too many cases, English makes no sense at all.

Spelling tricks:

mnemonic devices*

The good news is there's a solution to this problem.

And no, it's not the spell-checker on your computer. For one thing, you don't always write on a computer. But even if you use a computer that has spell-check, you still have to check your work carefully, because spelling checkers don't catch everything. If you write, "I went too the store" or "I went two the store," the

---

* You know spelling is hard when the word that means "spelling tricks" is spelled *mnemonic*.

spelling checker might not notice anything is wrong because *two* and *too* are
both correctly spelled words.

No, the solution to the spelling problem is to use tricks. There are a whole bunch of little mental tricks to make those hard-to-spell words easy to remember.

Take the word *cemetery*. I used to have trouble spelling it, because it seemed like there should be an *a* in there somewhere. Then somebody told me that if you just imagine three tombstones in a row with the letter *e* on each one, you'll never forget that cemetery has three *e*'s. And she was right. I never did.

Here are a few tricks for other confusing words:

Together: Break it into three little words: *to*, *get*, and *her*.

Principle or **principal**? Which one is in charge of your school? Just remember this: the principal is your PAL.

Desert or **dessert**? Which one is the hot place with a lot of sand, and which one is a tasty treat after a meal? You always want seconds of a treat, right? So add a second *s* for seconds when you want to spell *dessert.*

Another great spelling trick is to learn a sentence in which the first letter of each word spells out a hard-to-spell word. So let's say you have trouble with the word *arithmetic*. No sweat! Just remember that **A** **R**at **I**n **T**he **H**ouse **M**ay **E**at **T**he **I**ce **C**ream. A-R-I-T-H-M-E-T-I-C!

Here are a few others you may want to try:

GEOGRAPHY:

George **E**astman's **O**ld **G**randmother **R**ode **A** **P**ig **H**ome **Y**esterday.

BECAUSE:

Big **E**lephants **C**an **A**lways **U**nderstand **S**mall **E**lephants.

RHYTHM:

Rhythm **H**elps **Y**our **T**wo **H**ips **M**ove.

NECESSARY:

Not **E**very **C**at **E**ats **S**ardines
(**S**ome **A**re **R**eally **Y**ummy).

OCEAN:

Only **C**ats' **E**yes **A**re **N**arrow.

LASAGNA:

Lasagna **A**nd **S**paghetti
Are **G**ood **N**utritional **A**ids.

PEOPLE:

People **E**at **O**ranges **P**eople **L**ike **E**ating.

BISCUIT:

Breakfast **I**s **S**emi-**C**omplete
Unless **I** **T**ravel.

PSYCHOLOGY:

Please **S**ay **Y**ou **C**an **H**elp
Old **L**adies **O**pen **G**reen **Y**ams.

If you go on the internet and search for spelling tricks, you'll find a zillion of these. Or you can invent your own. If you do, make them personally meaningful.

Let's say you always forget how to begin the word *beautiful*, and you have an annoying brother named Bobby. Just think, Bobby Eats An Uncooked Toenail, and form an image in your head of your brother biting his own toes. You'll never forget that *beautiful* starts with B-E-A-U-T.

Think up weird images, rhymes, or odd sayings that will stick in your head.

I before *e*, except after *c*, and blah blah blah blah blah blah blah blah blah.

You've heard this one before: *i* before *e* except after *c*, or sounding like *a*, as in *neighbor* or *weigh*.

This rhyme comes in handy, because there are so many words with an *ie* in the middle (*achieve, belief, mischievous*). The problem is that there are lots of exceptions to the rule: *either, neither, foreign,*

forfeit, height, leisure, seizure, caffeine).
And of course there's one very important
word that goes against this rule:

Weird.

Just to make things more confusing . . .

Some English words, called **homophones**, sound the same but are spelled differently and have completely different meanings. For example, *fare* and *fair*. You pay your bus *fare* to go to a county *fair*. If you get cheated, it's not *fair*.

You *wear* clothes, but if you lose your clothes you don't know *where* they are. (*Where* always refers to a place.)

You don't *here* with your ear, you *hear* with your ear. That's a simple way to remember it—the word *ear* is in *hear*.

Think about the words we discussed: *too*, *two*, and *to*; *affect* and *effect*. These are also homophones, so you can't spell them by sounding them out. You just have to remember them.

"A synonym is a word you use when you can't spell the other one."
—*Baltasar Gracián*

Secret
spelling trick . . .

Shhh, don't tell anybody that I told you this. Certainly don't tell your teacher. It's a secret just between us. Ready?

If you don't know how to spell a particular word, DON'T USE THAT WORD!

For example, let's say you're about to write this sentence: "It is unnecessary to go to Harvard to become successful in life."

The problem is, you're not quite sure how to spell *unnecessary* or *successful*. In fact, these are two very commonly misspelled words because of those repeating letters.*

Here's your solution: trash the sentence entirely and reword it. Such as: "You don't have to go to Harvard to make something of yourself."

Pow! Done! Simple!

---

* You could go look them up in a dictionary, of course. But that would involve effort, so forget about it.

If you can't spell the word you want to write, use another word! Rephrase the sentence. It works every time. And nobody will ever know you were just too lazy to look up *unnecessary* and *successful*.

Having said that, if you can't get up off the couch to check the spelling of a word, you are truly a lazy bum! You should be ashamed of yourself. It's not hard. They've got these things called dictionaries. Open one in print or online. It won't kill ya.

Bad words!

Here's a list of words that are notoriously hard to spell. Just to keep you on your toes, see if you can find the one word on the list that is *misspelled.** No words are actually misspelled

135

*meaing the actual word misspelled.

abbreviate

absence

accidentally

achieve

a lot

arctic

average

beautiful

beginning

belief

believe

bicycle

biscuit

broccoli

business

calm

chaos

congratulations

eight/eighth

embarrass

especially

exaggerate

February

foreign

fourth

fulfill

canceled

conscience

conscious

deceive

desperate

disease

encyclopedia

enough

Fahrenheit

genius

government

guarantee

handsome

height

heroes

illegal

immediately

irresistible

judgment

knowledge

laboratory

laugh

library

license

lieutenant

loneliness

miscellaneous

mischievous

misspelled ← *there you go!*

necessary

neighbor

occasionally

occurred

often

parallel

physical

piece

pigeon

possession

receive

rhyme

rhythm

schedule

separate

sincerely

succeed

thought

through

tongue

ukulele

unnecessary

vacuum

valleys

Wednesday

weird

xylophone

Did you find the one word on the list that was misspelled? It was *misspelled*.

So all of those words above are spelled right?

Yup! Ha! Nah-nah-nah boo-boo on you!

FINAL WORDS

Ouch! Words hurt!

They say the pen is mightier than the sword. But to be honest, if somebody was going to attack me, I would rather they do it with a pen.

The My Weird School books start off with the words, "My name is A.J. and I hate . . ." Every so often I get an angry email from someone who objects to the word *hate* and says using that word encourages hatred. One parent even tried to get the series banned from his son's school.

Personally, I don't feel that the word *hate* encourages hatred. *Hatred* encourages hatred. But the point is that words can make people happy, they can make people sad, and they can also make people very angry. You may write something that you think is funny, silly, or innocent, but somebody else may be deeply offended by it. You may find that your teacher (or your parents) don't approve of the words or the content of what you've written. That's another reason why you should read over what you've written very carefully.

You need to decide whether or not the words you've written might offend anyone, and whether or not that matters to you. Sometimes, you should go ahead and use the words anyway. In the end,

I decided to stick with "My name is A.J. and I hate . . ." because I thought those were the words A.J. would really use, so I start the books that way and only a few people have complained. I figure it's okay to offend a few very sensitive people if I can help millions of kids get excited about reading.

Learn from the masters

One way to improve your writing is to study great writers. Tom Wolfe is a wonderful adult author who has written many great books such as *The Right Stuff* and *The Electric Kool-Aid Acid Test*. I'd like to quote from his 1987 bestseller *The Bonfire of the Vanities.* On the first page of the story, he wrote:

"Heh-hegggggggggggggggggghhhhh-hhhhhhhhhh!"

A few lines down, Wolfe wrote:

"They go, 'Hehhehheh...unnnnhhhh-hunhhh . . . That's right . . . Tell 'em, bro . . . Yo . . .'"

Then, a few pages later, Wolfe wrote:

"'Go on home! . . . Booooo . . . Yagggghhh . . . Yo!'"

And a little further on, he wrote:

"'Boooo! . . . Yegggghhh! . . . Yaaaggghhh! . . . Yo! . . . Goldberg!'"

You may think I'm making fun of Tom

142

Wolfe. I'm not. He's one of my favorite authors. As you go through school, you're going to learn the rules of grammar. Your teacher may tell you never to begin a sentence with the word *and* or end it with a preposition. You'll learn lots of other rules of the English language.

I hope your teachers will also tell you that the greatest writers, artists, and musicians were not the ones who followed all the rules. They were the ones who *broke* them for a purpose! Being creative means doing things *differently* from the way they have always been done before. Following rules perfectly is easier than breaking them creatively. I would argue that it's more important to communicate an idea or message than it is to follow a bunch of rules.

So go ahead. Break some rules. But you have to know them first. And don't write,

"Heh-hegggggggggggggggggghhhhh-hhhhhhhhhh!"

Because Tom Wolfe beat you to it.

"A story should have a beginning, a middle, and an end . . . but not necessarily in that order."
—Jean-Luc Godard

Texting as a second language

I'm going to end this book with a few words about texting. A lot of you have cell phones and use them to swap text messages with your friends and family. Obviously, it's easier to type **CUL8R** on that tiny keypad than it is to type **See you later**. It's easier to write **nite** than **night**. I know it's a nuisance to switch back and forth between capital and small letters when you're texting. Nobody would expect you to use perfect grammar, punctuation, spelling, and complete sentences in a quick text to tell your mom that you'll be home in five minutes.

The problem is that a lot of kids will

come to school and continue writing as if they're sending texts. They'll abbreviate all the words. They won't use punctuation. They'll avoid capital letters. Or they'll write in all caps. It drives teachers crazy.

I'm going to tell you something that will blow your mind: You are multilingual.

Do you know what that means? It means you know more than one language—text language and formal language. When you're in school, put the text language aside and switch to formal language. Put a capital letter at the beginning of each sentence and a period at the end. Spell every word correctly. Write complete sentences. Use commas, question marks, quotation marks, and exclamation points when they are needed. Not only will your teacher be happy, but you will be communicating your ideas clearly. If you just use your text language *all* the time, you're going to look like a dumbhead in school. But fortunately, you're smart enough to speak two languages.

See? You didn't know you were so talented!

Measure twice, cut once

That's a wise saying used by carpenters. It means that you should measure a piece of wood *very* carefully before you cut it with your saw. Because after you cut it, you can't put it back together again if you made a mistake. The same can be said for texting, emailing, and posting material online. Once you hit that Send button or Return key, you can't take it back. If there are dumb mistakes, false information, or embarrassing content, too bad! And remember, that message you dashed off without thinking might get printed out, forwarded to a million strangers, or posted *anywhere*. So always read and reread your messages—preferably out loud—before you send them.

"Proofread carefully to see if you any words out."
—William Safire

Well, it looks like we've reached the end of this book.* Before I send it to Harper-

---

* I *hope* this is the end, because there aren't many pages left after this one. It would be weird to keep writing a book after the pages run out.

Collins, I'm going to put it aside for a week or so. Then I'm going to read the book over again several times, just to make sure I corrected all my mistakes and made it as good as it could possibly be. I'm going to read it out loud and pretend I'm somebody else. Oprah, maybe. My wife, Nina, is going to read it, too. So will my daughter, Emma. They always catch a few mistakes that I missed. Finally, Andrew, my editor at HarperCollins, is going to read it. If you find any mistakes in this book after all those eyes have gone over it, heads are going to roll!*

It would make sense to finish with the

---

* Andrew's!

one tip that will improve your writing more than anything else. Are you ready? Okay, here it is. . . .

I'm not going to tell you.

Okay, okay, I'll tell you!

The tip is simple: READ! Read, read, read! If you want to be a better writer, read everything you can get your hands on. Read like crazy!

Maybe someday, I hope, I'll be reading *your* books. That would be cool.

"Increase your word power. Words are the
raw material of our craft. The greater your
vocabulary the more effective your writing."
—P. D. James